risen

risen

mandy precious

Mandy Precious (signature)

the bad press

Published in 1998 by
The Bad Press, PO Box 76, Manchester M21 8HJ

ISBN 0 9517233 8 3

All rights reserved.
Copyright Mandy Precious 1998
A CIP catalogue record for this book
is available from the British Library.

1 3 5 7 9 2 4 6 8

Cover designed by Robert Cochrane.
Cover photographs by Phil Chatterley.
Author photo by Karin Albinsson.
Author as a child courtesy Precious family archive.

Printed by The Arc & Throstle Press Limited
Nanholme Mill, Shaw Wood Road, Todmorden, Lancs OL14 6DA

ACKNOWLEDGEMENTS

Magazines:
*Other Poetry, Scratch, Sinister Wisdom (USA),
Prop, Krax, Affectionate Punch, Aireings,
Brando's Hat, Body Ornament, Psychopoetica*

Books & Anthologies:
*Life's Tupperware Party (Crocus)
Feeding the Bi-valve (Blue Nose Poetry Anthology98)
Urban Love Poetry (A.K.Press)
Something Piggy and Unappealing (Graft)
Cardigans and Gerbils (Hot Fish Press)*

Tape:
Begin Here (The Word Hoard)

Exhibitions:
*Body Ornament (NW Arts/Design Maker Network)
Wastelands (with the help of a NorthWest Arts Bursary)*

Other Media:
Granada Television, BBC Radio

A very special thank-you to Liz Kirby

Contents

First Born	09
Surburban Nightmare	10
Spreads From The Hips	12
Mrs And Mrs Jones Into Battle	14
Border Crossing Patrol	15
Idle Tattoo	16
Examination	17
Pride And The Sea	18
Gone With The Wind	19
Betty	20
Cliff	22
A Letter To Mr Greenfield	23
Life Story	24
Noel	27
Good Riddance To Bad Rubbish	28
Arson Attack	29
She Will Be coming Back Soon	30
Risen	31
Out Of The Box	42
Damian And Shelley	53
Friday Nights In	54
Michaela	55
Trigonometric Functions	56
Closure	58
Nightmare: Kerry Martin's Chest	59
Ian: That Was Then, This Isn't	60
Norma	61
In the Air Over Lithuania	62
Skeleton Woman	63

'Mandy Precious' poetry mainly concerns itself with outsiders, from the lonely or disturbed to victims of prejudice to those whose lot is to observe life's leading players. Yet these are far from mereout-pourings of pity or the poetic equivalent of wailing and gnashing of teeth - there is genuine art in the poems' humour, ironies, solid structures, inventive and telling images.'
Steven Blyth, Prop

Do I contradict myself? Very well then,
I contradict myself. I am large.
I contain multitudes.
Walt Whitman

Follow your inner moonlight,
don't hide the madness.
You say what you want to say when
you don't care who's listening.
Allen Ginsberg

To Mary

First Born

I was wearing the wrong suit.
The colour was too strong.
It was a cotton in a world of polyester.
My hair was too short. It should have been long
or highlighted, or hot brushed, or back-combed.

I was saying the wrong words.
Sensible words like: five children under six is about
four too many. They went down flat like
the champagne for the first baby.
I was living the wrong truth, in my flat-heeled,

sensible shoes. I was too slim, too trim,
unmothering. Then, I stopped being invited to
the Christenings, a thing I tried to mind.
I knew my sister shared round chicken paste
sandwiches, as she did with tears,

at the first baby's funeral.
And I was vegetarian.

Suburban Nightmare

In the silence of suburbia
she is angry that he has had
a heart attack during *Neighbours*.
He said, *"Toadfish's face is more frog-like."*
Meanwhile, her emphysema breathing speed
increased, having missed a crucial line.
She turned to see him going green.

The hook, the cliff-hanger caught between them
like a kite in a tree. An episode.
No clean streets. No neat story lines.
Yesterday's rubbish from a cat attacked sack,
a pair of clackers high up on a telephone wires.
SOS sent. Not received.
Or else down the wires lost in a ditch,
that carry word to her sister
without a hitch except she lives
the other side of town and isn't in.

Everything caught between them.
She is on the street looking for the old woman
who plays out her own death,
re-lives her stroke for millions
or a teenager with a painfreepregnancy
or the boy, too simple for a Special School.
They are all gone. Silence.
They are all in. Watching *Neighbours*.

She imagines there is a camera in the sky,
recording her life,
taking shots at all angles,
to be beamed across continents
to another world where water goes backwards.
She will rewind,
and he will wake up in the nick of time
in a bloodless hospital which beeps.

In the silence of suburbia,
there is weeping.

Spreads From The Hips

She spreads from the hips,
straddles the last fifty years
in a queue, waiting for a ticket
to a special concert
that she's always last but one in line for:
empty-handed. Tom Jones sings
but she never hears him.
He gyrates but her pants
stay steadfastly full-mast.
She waddles home fatter than when
enthusiasm woke her.

He says in answer to everything:
"I am going fishing."

The fresh taste of enthusiasm kissed her lips, once,
gave her such tender joy.
She would have walked across
Anlaby Road blind-fold
if he'd asked her.

He is thigh deep in waders
catching fish to throw back in.

In the mornings,
the weight is over. He rolls into work
on a matter of principal; forgotten.
Days pass in silence.

Her life is a picture.
Words spin like *love* and *him* until
all that remains is:
"*How about chips for tea?*"

He has caught the biggest salmon in Yorkshire.
He leaves it on the bank
until it is too stunned to swim.

Too stunned by how the sums don't add up,
by how the queue always finishes
even if she gets there first.
She breathes deep than shallow.
She is the field he is leaving fallow.
Too stunned. Yesterday yielded
fairy cakes and spaghetti bolognaise
which they ate in silence.

Mr And Mrs Jones Into Battle

Two Round Heads live at the bottom
of our road. They live behind a torquoise
front door and appear normal.
For most of the week he lectures
in Human Biology at the Tec,
and she buys Shredded Wheat from *Netto*.

A problem arises at the weekend
that makes them almost Cavalier:
what to do with the baby?
Farm him out to sitters
or risk Cromwell's chagrin again
by pushing a *Mothercare* pram into battle.

Border Crossing Patrol

"*Which Country?*" she asks
pointing at the Rainbow Flag
with its plastic mast,
and its nasty gold end bit,
my lover's attached to the dash
with *Blue Tack*.

She's told me about her diabetes.
Details of her life as an evacuee in Cumbria.
The berries she stole as a child,
the lies she told.
She walked on the wild side just once.
She doesn't open her front curtains in the day.
Her daughter-in-law calls her a vampire.
Blood-sucking information gatherer,
border patrol.

"*No Country,*" I say,
thinking nothing contains what we are.
Flying a flag no-one recognises but
our own kind; sliding over
border lines unnoticed.

IDLE TATTOO

'Uck
He wore a salmon pink plaster
over the 'F' on his forehead.
He thought we wouldn't guess
what 'UCK stood for.

Blue Dot
He took to wearing his mother's
face paint, *Ivory Coast*,
to hide the Blue Dot
and his borstal history.
By day's end the ghost
of his time inside rose again.

Fudging Lines
As he aged,
the tattoos bled blue into his arms,
fudging the lines, distorting pictures.

Lines were often blurred.
He rarely discerned the difference
between mother and daughter.

Examination

We're silent for so short a time, intense
concentration after years of learning.
It's a glance, a thing balanced with longing.
You're tempting as Belgian chocolate,
unwise as good wine in the afternoon.

In a second, I am assessed by you,
a possibility in the easy
multi-choice. Later, a weighty quote on
Paper Two, with DISCUSS in caps,
a problem that requires planning, execution.

I've done my revision. I can walk past
your tight yellow jeans, your perfect
gelled hair, eyes as mad as rabbits in Spring.
I have passed this test before
when I needed my soft heart breaking.

But you. You demand attention. You are
like the boy with the rag doll hair,
who loaded his nose with pencils and
filled his head with their lead, one clean bang to
his brain, rather than fail. You're desperate.

Pride And The Sea

Mother said I should be proud
but I seem so small
and you so big, sea.
She says, I should walk tall
in me best dressed England Kit
even though we didn't make it
to the Final and Brazil did.
But all I can think of is
how I'd like to race through the waves
and crash into the caves you've created.
Mother says I'll get me shoes wet
but I know, sea,
you are more important than Nike Air.
Sneakily, I announce I am looking for crabs,
but really I want to witness the sand
filling the gaps under rocks
just as fast as father knocks me.
Mother says I do look smart
whatever father says, sea.
She says I look grand
and father's no heart or soul...
But there's a big hole in me
and nothing seems to fill it,
except maybe running along the beach,
with my name on the wind,
well out of my parents' reach.
Then, I'm almost proud, sea,
because you are all around me,
and you feel like freedom,
and you feel like family to me.

Gone With The Wind

I was a bit part in the drama he was writing.
I should have been the star,
but I was afraid of his direction.
So, I missed the odd rehearsal.
Threw a tantrum or two.
It would have been fine if he'd kept to
the contract we'd signed.

The result of our minor misunderstanding was:
I ended up with a walk-on role,
the perfectly executed cameo:
a quick bow at the back of a famous cast,
the last to be asked for an autograph.
I didn't mind, it was all good experience for
THE BIG ONE - opposite a beautiful soul.
Who said, "Macbeth?"

He begged me to take the lead in his next
big production. I declined. He appointed
himself my agent, with total control.
(I forgot to read the small print.)
So, I am a bad named actor, booked only
for adverts and the odd naked pose.
That's show business.

Bang go my dreams of a BAFTA
for my classic, highly acclaimed
leading lady in a romance.

Betty

"Viv Nicholson works in a Supermarket now,"
she says, her laboured breathing,
                              short, a count down.
Viv was proper rough, went to the local
not in shoes, but bare-feet, fluffy pink slippered.
Viv's mouth was a sewer, rich with expletives.
They both worked the mill, like all of them until
the earth jerked, made her ill and Viv Nicholson
a pools winner. Viv spent her big bucks on,
of all things, a Pink Cadillac, driven through
Castleford with the roof right down when
it was raining and race horses that never won.
Spent it all, every penny of it, Viv Nicholson,
famous for fifteen minutes.

Spent it all, what would have been millions now,
and then, enough to live in comfort until
her dying days. She coughs, laughs,
                              doesn't blame Viv,
or mind her own rough luck, breathes faster
not even a million seconds left.
She coughs hard, her navy blue jogging suit,
hanging off coat hanger arms, when she's run
nowhere in her life, not even from home.
Left her mother's to move in down the road
with her damaged baby and it's been
twenty years without her husband and no cash.
She could never win. Her twin's Alzheimer's.
Things. She has never complained.

She just reads biographies and watches *Keyhole*
things that detail famous lives, like Viv Nicholson's
who was one of them.
Breathing hard, she says,
a sharp intake to get it out, staccato:
"Viv said, if she lived her life again,
                              she'd do the same.
Spend, spend, spend...."
She doesn't know: imagines.

Cliff

I used to throw soil 8'2" boots thick with clay.
It wasn't just digging holes
or seeing bodies and bones cracked.
It was like any other job,
like being an engineer and that.
I can't say I was shocked, mostly bored
by the many different ways people go
and all that crying.

I've seen ladies mascara run so many times.
I've lost count. Men: being stiff and tough.
Children playing with flowers,
running wild between the aisles of graves.
I'm not that brave.
I've stood aside and cried
when babies never got a chance.
Watched mothers felled like a tree, with grief.
It tested my belief. In God.
I never saw Him down the hole with me.

Vicars try,
but there's too much dying in the end.
I'm going just the same.
I'd like to meet the man who digs the hole
I'll be folded into.
I'd like to shake the hand of the man
who takes the dead flowers away,
and keeps the hedges trim.
I'd like to give him a Christmas tip.

A Letter To Mr Greenfield

Dear Mr Greenfield
if you should read this
please don't hesitate to
forward the letters you are so
kindly holding.

I should like to know
the result of my smear test
in the summer of 1994.

I wouldn't mind seeing
the photographs my father took
of Whitby Abbey.
You can keep the one's of my mother
in her bikini,
my need is probably less great than yours.

If you should receive my latest
telephone bill,
feel free to pay it immediately.

LIFE STORY

Transvestites of Life
We were caught in the wrong bodies,
transvestites of life.
She wanted everything I hated:
attention, bigger breasts,
a man's breath on her neck.
I wanted the steady pace of the 800 metres,
she trained for nightly.
She wanted to lose her virginity.
I coveted her spikes,
her athlete's coloured tights
and the easy, unsullied life
of the pace-maker.

Dream On
Crashing the car
I realise how far
I have slipped,
how low I'm unzipped
in a world where
I know no end and
no beginning
only fantasy spinning
through the axis.

I should take taxis.

30 Things
Of the thirty things, I was meant to do
before I reached thirty two,
there are some, like getting rid of you,
I can't remember learning how to
or if I did at all
or if they just got done
by dint of fortune or bad luck.
But one, I've stuck at and I've studied
and can do with ease...that is, of all the frogs
I've kissed and all the chances I have missed,
I'm pleased to say I can,
above and beyond all this,
hail a taxi with aplomb.

Expletive
Strange how in your mouth
it reels like an expletive:
LESBIAN? you said,
as if you really meant it.

Postcards (It's a small world after all)
I'm stuck by the words you wrote to me
on our fourth anniversary:
written to your previous lover.
The same double women's sign in red ink,
for this other woman
who made you think
you'd found true love
and it never died, although it did...

on the back of a postcard entitled:
"*The Tomb of The Unknown Housewife*"
an old girlfriend of mine designed.

The Story of My Life (it's only short without you)
When it's rewound,
they'll discover something profound:
she is the same both ways.

When it's replayed
as a contemporary dance,
she'll keep the steady pace.

When it's remade
as a melodrama,
she'll be the only thing in colour.

Noel

His life was left here, in the lean-from,
a railway man's cap, 'Noel' printed in an unsteady
hand.
Clothes grown bored with and out of.
Bicycles, tools, a tube of *Super Glue*.
Nothing really.

Inner tubes. Hundreds of inner tubes, fragmenting
apart from stubborn mended patches.
The picture of a woman smiling through a cracked
frame.
An aerogramme from Mrs Smith in Jamaica, '76,
complaining that Noel left and left nothing really.

So many inner tubes, wide and black,
for two *Chopper* bicycles, left too,
a wheel missing and front forks twisted.
I understand how it happens. The clues to him
like a nasty bruise. Nothing really.

Noel was proud of the security light we don't use,
the yellowing walls we paint over. Glad of the hugs
of the white woman (a smiling polaroid behind the
wardrobe).
She said she loved him, a skeleton of blue ink,
fading.
It came to nothing. Really.

Good Riddance To Bad Rubbish

He didn't do anything - except once
he shovelled snow. He cleared a whole road.
It kept falling and falling and falling.
He gave it up as a bad job, like all things.

He collected the stuff that people throw,
went on clandestine visits to the tip.
Not the one his wife was found on: another.
He shouted, "Good riddance to bad rubbish."

His wife was dead. Better that than prison
which is where, before the last overdose,
she'd been: two years for selling a daughter...
cheap at half the price, a good bargain deal.

He didn't do anything. But once
he'd come in and seen, and seen nothing wrong
with his daughter on Dick the Dustman's knee.
She kept falling and falling and falling.

Something in his daughter died in all this,
her mother taken, then her taken too;
dumped in a home like the stuff people throw.
He said, "Good riddance to bad rubbish."

Arson Attack

First I saw my mother's face:
lined with pain,
the sand in a timer turned.
She curled her nose, swayed.
The smoke came.

I thought of my brothers, Russian dolls,
two in a matching set of three,
still asleep. And me, the first born,
features just the same as
Mother-Father crossed.

No minutes remained.
She screamed, came to push
me through the window.
I was the man of the house.
Through thick smoke,
I pushed her.
Her legs broke.

Mam's tears came fine and fast as truth.
We both knew, in that last glance,
when I turned to save the other two.
Every grain of sand went through my hands.
Her head went back, a scream of pain.
The flames came.

She Will Be Coming Back Soon

It is like they have argued and she is
looking everywhere for something
to occupy her to make him sweat.
He remembers the words of rows.

It is like her car has broken down
on the hard-shoulder
and the *AA Membership* has lapsed
because he forgot to post the letter.

It is like she is desperate to find
that dress that will impress him
and she is wandering through town.
She cannot return without it.

It is like she has met her friend in the
village and they chat about
a juicy piece of gossip
and have forgotten the time.

She will be coming back soon.

Risen

He understands some things.
He knows the shape and texture of his hands.
He knows the smell,
rich as chocolate cake,
of his sculptured body.
Sometimes, when he sees the
thin brown of his skin,
he knows perfection.
one two
counting
one two
He knows how many reps
to pound in the gym.
Up down one two
Sometimes he thinks
there aren't other numbers
one two
her him
He knows himself.
Understands some things.

When he arrives,
the lights are off, muscles resting.
A museum is the earth's core: eye's shut.
Taut as the night. It's dark, coal pit black: hard.
Thick. He knows she watches him.
He is in the small room at the back,
knocking a secret code
into a box. *one two*

The air is still, rare as birds in winter.
It smells of yesterday's sandwiches,
cheese and onion crisps,
old men's feet.
An unsteady, syncopated heart beat.

A narrow shaft of light points like
his mother's gnarled fingers
at the glass case.
Everything points to it. The core.
Like the tightness of his abs.
Spaghetti junction.
Air-traffic control.

He is William Shankley,
Robert Paisley,
Joseph Fagan,
Kenneth Dalglish.

He is one in a long line of men
with minds that understand some things.
It's a jock-strap socialism.
The smell of male bodies. Armpits.
A hotline to goal,
the deep green of football fields,
the call of the crowd.
Stuff that makes men cry.

He does not understand her.

Points at the glass case.
He walks to her:
a single step across the hollow hall,
each step the shape a piece of cake:
a perfect wedge shape.
He fixes the light above her head.
She seems tight, an angel. Bright.
He watches her, almost wax.
Serene: good enough to eat.
She is pure white: gleams
like a porcelain bath freshly wiped.

He is Rodney Stewart,
Reginald Dwight,
David Bowie,
Michael Jagger.

He is one in a long line of men
with minds that understand some things.
It's an electric guitar socialism.
The sway of time,
a way to make words rhyme,
find each other.
Shape to move people to hysteria.
the rancid smell of joy. Soul.
Stuff that makes men cry.

He does not understand her.

He unlocks padlocks from the inside.

She waits, unshifting.
The door spins.
It's like a child's top with a dodgy pin.
Maroon door jamb, a fat old man,
sandwiches glass still unclean from
yesterday's hoards:
a class of National Curriculum five year olds.
A spell is cast.
It is the sound of breaking glass.

The red stripe on his tie
is knotted by a hand unused
to undoing things.

He is Eric Morecambe,
Anthony Hopkins,
Thomas Cooper,
Richard Emery.

He is one in a long line of men
with minds that understand some things.
It's a punchline socialism,
the giddy heights of laughs
rolling down hills like children.
The red of a fez, the wonk of glasses,
a hounddog, a "Ooh, you are awful!"
The deep crimson of mouths wide.
Stuff that makes men cry.

He does not understand her.

He rolls the sleeves of his navy jumper,
reveals biceps, hard-worked in the gym:
folded impatiently, a perfect figure of eight,
an indigo tattoo,
the name of a girl he can't remember.
He waltzes to her partnerless.
He steps to her, a centre piece,
centre folding.
She catches a glimpse of the green and blue
pencil thin stripe on his sock
freshly laundered with Ariel.

Any space encloses.
The walls move in.
His dreams are coloured by her,
and the municipal cream of his surroundings.

He is Valentino,
Charlton Heston,
Steven McQueen,
John Travolta.

One in a long line of men who
understand some things.
It's a celluloid socialism.
The look of an eye,
the train of a romantic smile.
The delivery of a single line
like Pizza to the starving.
How to lie.

Stuff that makes men cry.

He does not understand her.
She is lying still in the glass cabinet.
Waiting.
There is orange silk beneath her.
She is lonely as the woman in *Safeway*
demonstrating.
Arranged like a bride's bouquet.
She sends out a high pitched wail,
an animal thing
only he can hear.

he counts
one two
sweeps up
hopes that
people
will not
come or
else he
will be
able
to wait
contain
himself
one two

There is musak...toilet music,
the stuff that dreams are made of.
He polishes the glass with *Mr Sheen*,
'til he can see his face in her.
She reflects him like a stream.
She is red: hot.
She is red hot.
She is red. Eyes, heart, limbs.
He imagines it is thoughts of him.

When the crowds come,
he counts them in.
click click one two one two
an insect trapped in a match box

She is ready for them.
He is not.
Some come really close.
He hates these. Hates them
with pain like the burning sensation
of lactic acid build up.
They press red noses,
red mouths, red lips to the case.
She waits: seems to flick a recalcitrant hip
as if to say "You're timid as deer at
                        Dunham Massey".
She likes to see the shake, the shock,
the cool Rock Hudson way
some stay looking.
Others twitch: finely made like a feather
or chiselled cheekbone.

It is fire to his eyes.

He is Aristophanes,
William Shakespeare,
William Gilbert,
William Russell.

He is one in a long line of men
with minds that understand some things.
It is a well rehearsed socialism.
The reek of words caught up in
a grid-locked pen.
Overweight tragedy,
Slimfast comedy.
Poetry-voice-poetry-voice.
Stuff that makes men cry.

He does not understand her.

He coughs.
It is calm and urgent at the same time.
He is a man who wants the taste of
Lucazade sport on his tongue.
Her.
He is delivering a monologue.
He steps through the fourth wall.
Silence. He waits. He wants.
He must have this thing.

As the crowd leave,

he takes off his clothes.
He is Shirley Bassey's little brother.
He runs from one end of the gallery to the other.
Hunter. Neanderthal.
Lemmy. Slash. Guitarman.
She is watching him.
His heart beat sounds like Big Ben.
It is as if she is laughing at him.
He might be an exhibit.
He could lie here, still as rock,
muscles pulled in.

one two
one two

He sweeps away outer wrappers
of *Kit Kats, Riley's Chocolate Rolls,
Kodak* film wraps.
He sweeps away bits of conversation
left at edges. Hanging.

He is Jack the Ripper,
Reginald Christie,
Peter Sutcliffe,
Fredrick West.

He is one in a long line of men
whose minds understand some things.
It is a wicked socialism.
The sweet taste of taking without asking.
The smell of fear.

The weight of secrets, needing, words,
of things long not said. Alone:
it's that child in the playground.
Stuff to make men cry.

He does not understand her.

She is still there. In there.
Still, still.
Sugar in the lemonade.
She hears the last click, click.
one two
one two
2,354 punters in one day
2,354 who have seen her naked,
white, naked as a wedding cake just iced.

There is the gleam of his sports socks
against sunbed brown.
No-one will know.
He lifts the lid,
sees her smile.

It is, he thinks a fireworks display.
A hat trick. A clever bridge.
A funny line. A sultry smile.
A first night.
Ejaculation.

A rocket. A power socket
two shapes, shifting bulk
like giant German sausages.
A dummy and the incredible Hulk.

She poisons him.
He knocks a secret code
into the box: *one two one two*
unlocks himself, unloads his rocks.

Perhaps she saw it quickly.
What to do
coming at her like a paint brush
to a canvas: angry and maroon.

Formaldehyde
one two one two

He is Jesus Christ,
The Prophet Mohammed,
Guru Nanak,
The Buddha.

He is one in a long line of men
who know some things.

Out Of The Box

She is outside the box,
neck high in synthetic red fur
inside a metal bubble:
a sixteen valve British Racing Green Fiesta.
Waiting.

She is watching for him. He isn't in.
She is watching even paced stout
middle aged ladies pass his gate,
wearing a path to *Gregg's* and *Safeway*,
carrying square bags in navy and tan.
Bags like armour plates for varicose veins,
covered in support tights from the Fat Shop.
Walking past his house.
He will be coming soon.
She is watching.
She is keen-eyed, a fifteen year wait.
She knows her ultimate fate
if she isn't careful:
a 3/4 coat and a husband home late.

She is a *Jackie* problem page,
a *Bunty* cutout, a *Blue Jeans* Picture Story.
She is a copy of the *Woman's Weekly*
her mother forgot to confiscate.
She is the sum of what she's read.
She is the catalogue of things she's done instead.

The street is cold.

The ice on his front gatepost is
like tartar on teeth.
She moves her feet,
two pairs of *Marks and Spencer* socks
in *Caterpillars*: strong, neat, sensible,
still riled at the cost.
She would like to walk on heels
but cannot and never could then.

She is waiting.
The disguise of a gorgeous woman,
just in the back.
His last chance to see what he hasn't got.
An article from *Cosmo* on methods of attack,
on what colours match.
Directions on mascara,
advice on whether to pluck
or not.
Waiting.

It is dark. Dark as mornings ready for work.
Fiercely black as a Vicar's frock.
Black as the funeral trousers
she hasn't taken off.
Black as her pupils as she watched
her grandmother slip beyond
crematorium curtains.
Black as inside that box.
She is waiting. Any second now. He is coming.

He is talking to her in her head,
telling her stories.
He is behind the scenes, nagging as toothache,
telling her things she didn't want to know,
doesn't believe
and can never forget.

She is *Flowers in the Attic*,
battered and handed around class.
She is Enid Blyton's George,
and the *The Twins at St. Clare*:
she is the mystery that's solved
on the very last page.
She is the sum of what she's read.
The catalogue of things done instead.

She is time standing still.
She knows who she is, strong and controlled.
She can do things at will.
She is waiting for him.
Waiting.

The moment will pass when she waits long enough.

She is an article in the *Hull Daily Mail*,
he's never read,
two columns off The Ripper and a suicide.

He is not here.
She is waiting.

She feels the picture of a football team,
1983, from the *Sports Green*,
arms across his puffed up chest,
the photograph folded into careful creases
and tucked for years in the inside pocket
of a lilac vanity case.

She studies his face,
quite old then. He is held in store
with a letter from the *Beano*,
an official kissing licence,
and certificates that mark her birth and some tests.
She is proficient in cycling.
There's a photograph of David Wilkie
from the public baths swimathon
with the number 1471
over her right breast.
Things he doesn't know
and has never cared for.
She is going to tell him for once and all.

She is a well-thumbed copy of
The Orge Downstairs,
and Michael Moorcock's *Behold the Man*,
secreted in her black *Adidas* bag,
upstairs in her crisp white shirt,
tight to her rock hard breasts -
inside, oiled and slick, uncaressed.
Breasts, hard and painful,
just like tiny fists

that punch but can't fight.
She is the sum of what she's read.
A catalogue of things done instead.

He is talking to her in her head,
telling her things
when she wants him dead and gone.

She is waiting. Watching his house
fat as something made in *Lego*.
Counting the old ladies out,
counting them back,
weighed down with late night shopping.
Just then, she unfolds his face,
wonders if she'd recognise him in another place.
15 long years, waiting.

Unfolding:
a rough skeleton of what it was, then.
The paper fragile, thin,
after 15 long years of wearing out
her fingers, keen as Venus fly traps,
lethal as night caps.
She is waiting.

Just then, she sees for the first time,
the size, big as elephants, of his feet.
Feet that would spread the seas,
rarely please at the end of the day.
Overcomplicate - that's her: unseen.

Silent as gas she's been, but never deadly.
Until now. Count down.
She is waiting. Days lost.
She is ready at last to break the mould,
take hold, stake it out on a cold winter's night
and arrest it for loitering.
She knows,
knows ever line on her hands,
every break of her heart.

He is talking to her in her head,
consigning her to restless nights.
He is walking her along a line
called insanity.

She is *Woman on the Edge of Time*.
She is lost in the mirror within.
She is caught between the pages of
Just like a Girl,
a quote highlighted in flourescent pink,
on an important page with the corner turned.
She is trapped in the headlights of
      Dworkin's *Pornography*.
She is the sum total of what she's read,
the things done instead.

She is waiting inside her car.
The outside air, sharp and cold
as a mother's scold.
It is dark, bleak as the days she's wasted
while he's tired of been dreamed.

If she takes him away. Beat.

Her breasts are heavier now, like rain clouds.
One flick, one rhythmic tick and she is wet again.

She is *My Secret Garden* and *Women in Love*,
a *Macho Slut*,
afternoons of long baths and hand relief.
She is waiting for a single sign,
an unfinished line
to move slowly to completion.
She is waiting this time.
She won't go away.
She is the sum of what she's read.
This is what she'll do instead.

She was always waiting
to be someone else, at some other time.
Someone altogether new.
She maintained it for years, breathing in
instead of out. Stayed thin.
When her size was the one that let
the sides out.

She was always planning
a technicolour escape from herself,
not now.
She always wore the wrong size bra:
just in case she came first place in the race.

Not now.

She is waiting,
fingering the knife,
remembering every slice of bread she's cut,
and the rhyme of the farmer's wife,
sharp as the creases on his suit pants.
She always wore a mask
because she didn't like her face: not now.

She is waiting,
two car spaces away from a street light,
not seen. Yet. Not quite heard. Yet.
She is waiting.
He is talking to her in her head,
holding her hostage,
white tape over her eyes and mouth.

She is counting the times, the minutes
and the days, that she's wasted
because the man with the beard
made promises he couldn't keep,
consigned her to workaholism
and not enough sleep.
She is waiting,
engraving her name in the dash with the blade
she's made sharp for him.

She's both Oedipus and Jocasta,
a mythological disaster.
She is a case history,
a three inch entry in
The Encyclopeadia Britannica
on a strange unknown disease,
a passing reference in *Encarta* to freaks.
She is the sum of what she's read,
what she'll do instead.

She is a moment that never happened.

She is waiting through the early rounds
at the pub - through bluster and pints,
outside his home.
500 yards from the pub door,
he'll eventually emerge from.
Perhaps he is boring: predictable,
like many others have been.
She is imagining the flight path of the knife
as it curves into strikes,
as it leaves her gloved hand.

She is waiting.
Angry now, that she is waiting.

It is black as coal.
It is cold.
It is the past that has this stranglehold.
Still waiting.

Her legs have opened a thousand times,
but never then.
No loss of virginity but innocence gone.
No standing ovation or
clever rotation of hips, nothing tangible.
It isn't hate she feels for him.

He is talking to her in her head.
He is always talking about coming.
Always coming a metaphorical mountain,
but never does, never arrives, never comes.

The road is silent, still
but for a passing car
and a marmalade cat
left out on a window sill.

She undoes the car door:
makes to wait closer,
recognises every inch of his gate post.
Sees herself in the plate glass of his front door.
Half eleven, the time moves slow.
He will never know what has hit him.
She won't be waiting anymore.

She is ready for him,
as he rounds on the path,
a little unsteady after the last glass.
She raises her hand,
lands her first blow, his mind ticking over

without recognition.
She doesn't know how many times
but counts twenty four.
She watches him bleed. Leaves.
Silent.

She is a final chapter, roughly torn.
He is talking to her in her head.

Damian And Shelley

We met between the weight machines
at *Stretford Leisure Centre*;
impressed each other with muscles and stamina.
He flexed his fast twitch, sipping isotonic orange
and I was smitten.

Later, we kissed, and he lifted me cleanly
against the passenger door of my A reg, red *Sierra*.
I'd dreamed of this in double mathematics
behind Murray Clarke,
whose feet smelt but was otherwise perfect.

For years, I have shaped this body for true love.
Sculptured it for incalculable hours,
as I punish the *Jogmaster*. No pretty countryside
for me to jog in, just mirrors to watch his like
develop *Weider* perfection. We've found it together.

We work at sweat in equal measure, a courtship,
stepping in unison and counting reps of ten,
breathe and then again. We love the power of
well-toned arms, entwined: thrusting
                              weights forward,
behind. We are committed to being perfect forever.

Friday Nights In

A big trampoline bed in my parents' room,
a tuck, a pike and a forward roll,
heart beating like feet on lino.

I catch sight of the girdle, off white.
It's hard plastic snaps still holding
American Tan stockings.

Any moment they might come back.
I-spy the catch for a secret drawer
on the walnut dressing table.

Unable to resist, I click the drawer wide
so I can see straight in.
They will return soon from *Dee's Discount*.

I fight the urge to flight.
I see what I don't quite understand:
slim, bright packages sealed with the word

'Featherlite'. I know enough to know
I've stumbled on it. Why I'm sent to
Gran's on Fridays. Why I'm an accident.

Michaela

My mother called her
'nothing more than a vegetable,'
so I imagined her green or maybe
carrot shape like she'd got in
a time-machine with a parsnip.
An amazing transformation
or something weird in a dream,
because she'd been beautiful.
Porcelain skin, deep eyes I'd got lost in
and hair so dark it could have come from
a *Cherry Blossom* tin.

When my mother said, in a hushed voice
'They've put her body up for research.'
I imagined a giant cabbage in a cage,
like a rabbit or a beagle smoking.
I imagined the incisions they made.
It was easier to think of her chopped
if she wasn't real, only green
or a bit pale and frilly round the edges.

Trigonometric Functions

I was lined up at a right angle to her
before either of us knew about
cosines and tangents.

I didn't die, had to suffer the indignity
of trigonometry without her.
A matter of millimetres.
Her tumour crossed an angle between
wicked and benign.
My slashed thigh
a rotation through the axis,
off a main artery.
I tried to learn by rote
how reciprocal relations
ctn A = 1/*tan A*,
sec A = 1/*cos A*,
csc A = 1/*sin A*,
but it meant nothing.
How she died and I didn't.

There was no flimsy orange pamphlet,
the spine worn from a thousand hands,
where I could trace the solution with a ruler,
record the answer carefully
in a fresh square,
marked right with a star and a tick.
Just a clumsy scar.

It was all crosses
next to unworkable equations.

It was Mrs Tuton asking, after she'd explained
why I still didn't understand.
It was how if the point Q
on the terminal side of angle A,
has standard co-ordinates (x and y)
(me and her)
this point will have co-ordinates
(x and - y)
(me minus her)
on the terminal side of $-A$
in standard position.

From this fact and the definitions
are obtained identities.
She died and I didn't.

Closure

Mother wore turquoise check overalls,
wrapping herself away from the world,
disguising her figure, her taste in clothes.
From the neck,
an apology of a polo-top,
hiding what remained of her body.

Once, in error, the heat of Scarborough
prompted her to remove layer after layer.
The whiteness, shocked me and
the sun which burned her like an
unpricked, thick pork sausage.

She only emerged this once.
Afterwards, whatever the weather,
she remained fiercely closed off,
as if her body held deep secrets,
messages it would disclose forever
with any minute exposure.

Nightmare: Kerry Martin's Chest

Nightmare. Heart beating fast.
The last empty chair,
the only one spare in the class:
the ultimate space, a final frontier, crossed.
A failure in the race,
a conspiracy so vast. A simple fact,
no-one likes me.

A realisation so shitty
it is equal only to Kerry Martin's laugh,
and her over-large chest,
and white crimpolene cardigan.
I must spend a year, near enough to touch.

She greets me with a knowing smile, it says
You, like me, will never be like the rest.

It's all too much.
The history of my unwashed grey vest
coming home to roost, my off-white knee socks,
all the things I'd been at pains to minimise.
I look around, they despise me.
They can feel my shame
at wearing knickers two days.
the nightmare of having P.E. then games.
They are saying:
Never forget, you do not belong here.
We do not like you.

Ian: That Was Then, This Isn't

Twelve years since our last encounter,
he ignores me again.
His *Adidas Mamba* are the same,
come full-circle. His thick lips, moustachioed,
unkempt hair: his boyish charm, now grown.

I always avoid him and Pud and Rink,
football crazy cases who fancied Man U
because the only good thing about Hull City
was the *Safeways* under the main stand.
The football never unimproved.

He sees the Big Piece drinking in *The Independent*.
He leafs through *The Sun*, flicks to the back page,
reads the stars, checks his lottery numbers
against his card, re-arranges his tackle,
leg wide, skims the headlines.

I say nothing, tense, sense the danger.
Do not tempt fate.
His knuckles blue with love and hate.
He reads the advertised colour change of *Pepsi Cola*.
I know it tastes the same.

Norma

I remember the siren
when she was already dead.
The smashed up mirror
she used as a weapon.
She tore gouges in her arms
deep as *Dane's dyke*.
We didn't believe it.

The blue light filled the street.
Her home winking in the sunlight,
a half shut eye, just kidding.

In The Air Over Lithuania
For Wendy Ingham

The old atlas recorded Russia
as though nothing changes much.
Landscapes wear away, trust

I trace the fine line between Latvia
and Lithuania: a point somewhere above.
On one page, both countries are pink
like the alternate check on a *Tiny Tears'* dress.
On the next Lithuania is an ugly red,
angry as skin dipped in acid.

She is holding forth. Laughing loud,
around the damson mauve of her mouth.
She is chewing *Wrigley's*.
The rolled up white ball
like a pair of new pants in an early wash.

When she eats, she knows in seconds.
Sees her hands swell redder and redder,
bigger and bigger
like an unwanted pregnancy.
Her throat closes in.

She crosses the line
in the air over Lithuania:
can't breathe, throat worn thin.
Landscapes fading.

Skeleton Woman

Waves of words crash into rocks,
stronger than the colour blue.

I have fallen from the cliff
wearing the wrong shoes.

I am down here,
on the edge of a vast ocean,

a semi-colon on the horizon.
There is no sign.

Nothing buried deep
in the rocks like a fossil.

Just words. Endless words.
A scream caught on the wind.

I am painting the house in colours
more complex than time.

I am painting to say I have been here
and this remains from the story.

I am painting to make sense of life
and death and sex and space.

The paint washes away
with the incoming tide.

I have ballooned the legs
of my trousers to keep afloat.

Words come in waves.
I am painting an intricate SOS

I am painting words, eaten.
I am eating words, swallowing whole.

The waves break. The sea dense with weeds,
intense with a silence of syllables and sentences.

Nothing stems the flow.
The sea cleans the bones.